Economies and Industries: Insight into Africa's Economic Potential

Maximum Fredrick

Copyright © 2019 Maximum Fredrick

All rights reserved.

ISBN: 9781707752690

DEDICATION

To my parents, Fredrick and Theresa. It's impossible to thank you adequately for all you've done for me.

PREFACE

Africans yearn for economic upsizing. They wish for a developed society, although many are not clear how development impact societies. I have drawn Africans to conversation; Nigerians to a greater extent, during my trip to different states of the country in 2018. Quite a few understand the secret to economic growth for countries, and the role of citizens in the success stories of advanced economies. Young Africans today will become leaders tomorrow. The sad reality, however, is that many are unprepared. For long now, I've sought to reshape minds across the continent by connecting with millions of her citizens in writing, sharing my thoughts on pathways to industrialization and technological advancement, and how economic transformation can create wealth for African countries. I've been passionate about helping citizens see Africa from an economic perspective. Such an effort led to this book.

While technology has long been an area of interest for me, putting this work together haven't come easy. Weeks without sleep, and a significant deviation from my routine were some of the things I had to endure.

Being close to Prof Kingsley Moghalu taught me to perceive economic problems from the viewpoint of an economist. In nearly 2 years, I learnt so much, without which this book will not exist.

Years as a technology entrepreneur, knowledge of economics acquired by close association with Prof Kingsley Moghalu, and innate talent for leadership were important resources for this work.

Maximum Fredrick

(October 3rd, 2019), Abuja - Nigeria.

FOREWORD

Economies and Industries: Insight into Africa's Economic Potential by Maximum Fredrick is a book that yet gives hope that Africa may eventually emerge as a developed continent in the near future. As I read the book, and as a Nigerian, I thought of how greatly blessed we are with vast and diverse resources: all-year-round pleasant weather, arable lands, fresh water sources, oil and gas deposits, solid minerals, plentiful sunshine, and above all, a large and energetic human population. However, we have not been fair to the Giver of these blessings: we have wasted and keep wasting these resources through poor leadership which is incapable of critical thinking and a gullible and docile population.

The book gives a concise analysis of the problems and recommendations of steps to take to develop Africa in the shortest possible time. I am amazed at the audacity of the author as he delves straight into the Fourth Industrial Revolution fields such as artificial intelligence, fifth generation wireless technology, autonomous vehicles, robotics, nanotechnology, alternative fuel and energy systems, quantum computing, etc. which he recommends for Africa now, even when most African nations are struggling to catch up with the First Industrial Revolution. In my opinion, this is the way for Africa to go in order to compete effectively with the rest of the World; because the capabilities are there in terms of human and material resources.

I am enthused by this book in the sense that it has rekindled my hope in Nigeria and Africa; that all is not lost: that somewhere, there are Africans with critical thinking who can turn around the current fortunes of Africa. I am enthused also by the fact that we can get a book of this nature from one of our youths who have generally been labelled as "yahoo boys". Maximum Fredrick is an undergraduate student of my University who has great entrepreneurial skills and political ambition. We are blessed to have youths like this. The least we can do is to encourage them to achieve their life's ambitions.

It is therefore on this note that I strongly recommend this book to African governments, political leaders, entrepreneurs, venture capitalists, political and social activists, youths, development experts and agencies, and lovers of African development. The book may look small, but it contains invaluable mine of ideas.

Akii Ibhadode, FAS, FNSE, FSESN, FMSTSN

Vice Chancellor and Shell Professor of Lightweight Automobile Engine Development

Federal University of Petroleum Resources, Effurun (FUPRE), Delta State, Nigeria

CONTENTS

Minerals in African Soil

Building Economies

The Move to Industrialization

Smarter Society

Africa's Growing Investment Market

Beyond Existing Government Model

Urbanization Strategy

The African Union

Agriculture: Pre-requisite for Raw Materials

Rivers and Economic Value: The Case of Africa

Today's Disruptive Technology

Racism Thrive Because No Black Nation is Successful

Global Economy Puzzle and Africa

A Note to Africa's Aspiring Entrepreneurs

INTRODUCTION

Technological revolutions have occurred universally. They have not only improved living standards and raised income levels, but have also impacted governments. Emerging technologies have created values-based leadership and have been used to adapt and modernize governance.

The first industrial revolution in the late 18th century caused a shift from mostly agrarian societies to greater industrialization brought by steam engine and other technological development. This ushered in mechanization of textile industries. The second industrial revolution of early 20th century created room for mass production as man mastered electricity and assembly lines. The third Industrial revolution brought about digitization. Manufacturing went digital with the rise of clever softwares, 3 dimensional printing and many other web-based services.

Industry 4.0, the fourth Industrial revolution promises great benefits as well as many potential dangers. Technologies emerging from fields like artificial intelligence (AI), fifth generation wireless technologies (5G), fully autonomous vehicles, robotics, nanotechnology, alternative fuel and energy systems, augmented reality (AR), quantum computing, biotechnology, the internet of things, the industrial Internet of things (IIOT), genome editing, decentralized consensus, and some others are reshaping the future. In many ways, developing countries such as we have in Africa tend to be slow in catching up with these developments.

"Economies and Industries: Insight into Africa's Economic

Potential" aims to provide direction for industrialization and technological advancement in Africa. It encompasses the continent's economic prospects, as well as suggests sustainable industrial structure for governments and entrepreneurs.

Chapter 1

Minerals in African Soil

"Africa needs robust geological data on their mineral deposits. Developing capacity in geological mapping should be a serious concern for Africans. Africa currently has very little data on rare earth metals in the entire continent"

Africa has the largest mineral industry in the world, resulting in an economy heavily dependent on mineral export, which has negatively impacted on technological growth in the continent. Minerals like Bauxite, a sedimentary rock with relatively high aluminum content, which is the world's main source of aluminum; Cobalt, a hard, lustrous silver-gray metal produced by reductive smelting; Diamond, which has the highest hardness and thermal conductivity of any natural material, with properties that are used for major industrial applications like cutting and polishing tools; Phosphate rock; Platinum-group metals (Iridium, Osmium, Palladium, Platinum, Rhodium, Ruthenium); Vermiculite and Zirconium are all abundant in Africa.

The 2012 share of world production provides the following statistics from African soil; uranium 18%; manganese 38%; mineral fuels (including coal) & petroleum 47%; bauxite 7%; chromite 38%; cobalt 60%;

platinum 69.4%; copper 9%; aluminum 5%; gold 20%; steel 1%; lead (Pb) 2%; zinc 1%; iron ore 2%; natural diamond 56%; graphite 2%; phosphate rock 21%; coal 4%; cement 4% [2012 Minerals Yearbook, US Geological Survey]. Other minerals are also present in quantities.

Foreign countries use minerals from African soil for manufacturing in industries. African countries can embrace industrialization too. The AU (African Union) must work to get member States set up policies encouraging industrialization if we are to attain prosperity. Algeria, Angola, Cameroon, Chad, Republic of Congo, Egypt, Eritrea, Gabon, Ghana, Kenya, Libya, Nigeria, South Sudan, Sudan, Tunisia, and Mozambique are oil-rich nations. At the boom in oil price between 2002 and 2007 when price nearly tripled, a Sovereign Wealth Fund should have been created by African countries with revenues from oil. This would have then been used to drive industrialization in the continent. Prices of mined minerals also nearly tripled during the era of oil boom, according to UN data, but this gain wasn't used in the interest of African countries as a whole. The world is fast drifting towards alternative fuel and energy sources; this raises concerns for countries that depend heavily on hydrocarbons like oil and natural gas.

Angola, Botswana, Central African Republic, and Democratic Republic of Congo have rich deposits of Diamond in their soil. Benin, Burkina Faso, Djibouti, Mali, South Africa, Tanzania have Gold. Burundi has Nickel and Uranium. Uganda and Zambia have Copper. Mauritania has Iron ore. Gambia has Titanium. Madagascar has graphite. Western Sahara and Morocco have phosphates. The list continues.

Countries in Africa have continually struggled to be economically productive, even with the presence of minerals in large quantities. World Bank's Chief Economist for the Middle East and North Africa, Shantayanan Devarajan, is of the same view. He wrote "It seems, that whatever the so-called developed world craves, Africa already has: from mineral resources to yet to be discovered deposits of diamonds, oils, and rare earths; to agricultural land. Yet, whatever enriches the so-called developed world from Africa seems to not benefit the continent itself. Why is that?"

As the world moves towards a low-carbon future, rise in green energy technologies will prompt an increase in demand for a wide range of metals and minerals. This will bring significant opportunities for resource-rich nations in Africa. Copper, lead, aluminum, manganese, nickel, lithium, silver, zinc, steel, and rare earth metals will be in high demand. Africa should forge long-term sustainable strategies for extracting these minerals and make sustainable investments.

Chapter 2

Building Economies

"Rapid and transformative growth are overseen by governments who are determined to mould their economies"

Developing industrial economies should be number one priority for African countries even though it is more of a challenge than it sounds. This is because to attract foreign investors, African countries need to become wealthier and build healthier economies. Asia is one continent that has experienced rapid technological breakthrough. They did that by having a clear, deliverable plan. Africa needs a plan too, perhaps quite different from those of successful Asian countries, because both continents have different demography.

Joe Studwell presents a readable analysis of what Asian countries did right and wrong that differentiates the stars from the rest in his book "How Asia Works"

Successful countries first carried out land reform. Smaller plots were broken off from estates owned by wealthier landlords and redistributed among rural households. This led to very labor-intensive agriculture that highly improved yields at a time when opportunities elsewhere were scarce. This reform helped maximize agricultural exports and boosted domestic consumption as well as savings.

Second, as laborers began to move out of agriculture, governments encouraged investment in industries that provided low-skilled work. This was combined with policies that encouraged manufacturers to export around the world and to keep moving up the value chain. While exporters were supported, unsuccessful ones went out of business as they were not cosseted by the government.

Third, financial sector was relatively tightly regulated by the government and focused on supplying credit to agriculture and then to successful manufacturing exporters. State influence was strengthened by capital control over the financial sector as well as insulate these economies from the ebb and flow of global markets. The above strategy worked for Asian countries, but the question is "What strategy has Africa?"

Emerging economies, unlike most developed economies, tend to have relatively young populations to power growth. This means there's an abundance of young workers and a shortage of retirees. And Asia's explosive growth was built on this demographic dividend. While these youthful demographics is important, they are not sufficient by themselves. Something else is necessary: without it youthful populations turn out to be wasted potential and a recipe for severe instability. There has to be a plan, and a will to execute it.

According to World Bank data, Japan had a GDP per capita of $480 back in 1960. Bringing in two benchmarks from other emerging regions, South Africa was on $430 and Brazil on $210. By 2017, Japan's GDP per capita had grown to more than $38,800, while South Africa stood at just $6,150 and Brazil at $9,800.

Japan may not be a fair standard to choose considering that it already had an industrial economy prior to World War II. So its recovery and boom after the war was in some respects a case of reconstruction rather than development, although its economy became far broader, more outward-looking and sophisticated. This however, certainly wasn't the case for South Korea. South Korea grew from a GDP per capita of $160 to $29,750 - higher than Greece and Portugal of European economy. Taiwan did almost as well. Until sustainable plans are laid to build industrial economies, African countries will continue to get it wrong.

Chapter 3

The Move to Industrialization

"As the world moves towards a low-carbon future, rise in green energy technologies will prompt an increase in demand for a wide range of metals and minerals. This will bring significant opportunities for resource-rich nations in Africa. Copper, lead, aluminum, manganese, nickel, lithium, silver, zinc, steel, and rare earth metals will be in high demand. Africa should forge long-term sustainable strategies for extracting these minerals and make sustainable investments".

Mining of minerals in the continent looks quite promising, and it is expected to remain so almost indefinitely. Governments however, should put away corruption and poor management of mineral resources by creating more transparency. Mining codes and contracts should also address environmental protection, adequate compensation to affected communities and the rehabilitation of land after mining operations have ceased.

Large mining operations in Africa have generated big profits for foreign companies, with little local benefit. To correct this, a resolve should be made leading to the establishment of private and State-owned mining companies operated by Africans. Proper management of extractive commodities can lead to two things for resource-abundant countries in Africa;

- Revenues from exports of minerals can be used to set up manufacturing industries, with these countries easily moving up the value chain as exporters of technological products.

- These countries would basically be self-sufficient in metals and minerals, and there would be no need to import to drive production in their industries.

Due to the influence of its vast oil resources, the mining of minerals in Nigeria accounts for only 0.3% of its GDP. Nigeria's domestic mining industry is underdeveloped and it results in Nigeria having to import minerals such as salt and Iron ore that can be produced domestically. This leaves Nigerians wondering what use is the Ministry of Solid Minerals Development. The world is looking towards a low-carbon future where rise in green energy technologies will prompt an increase in demand for a wide range of metals and minerals. Crude oil is gradually losing its value yet governments at this point are slow to realize it. The future doesn't look promising for oil. Mining of minerals will do much for countries in Africa.

In a Ministry of Planning publication dated 1983 (Page

58), the United Arab Emirates spoke of the rationale for industrialization in the country. UAE sought for diversification of an economy that is heavily reliant on oil. The publication reads *"Industrialization is a main aim of the state for the correction of the structure of production in which the crude oil sector accounts for about two thirds of the GDP. The industrial sector, according to economic criteria, is the sector on which economic efforts should be concentrated."* Contribution to GDP from non-oil sector rose from 36.73 per cent in 1980 to 77.64 per cent in 1998. The contribution of manufacturing also increased from 3.76 per cent in 1980 to 12.40 per cent in 1998. Even so, reliance on the oil sector is still high. But exporting refined rather than crude oil enables the UAE to benefit from the value-added component, which is not so in most African countries (if not all).

Agriculture should be sustainably modernized to serve as alternative path to revenue generation. Agriculture also creates market for complex manufacturing industries as machineries and equipment like tractors and ploughs are sold for mechanized farming. Lastly, it is important to remember that agriculture depends on mined minerals such as phosphates to fertilize the soil. A relationship therefore exists between mining and agriculture.

On Industrialization, providers of intellectual and physical capital - the innovators, shareholders, and investors, tend to be the largest beneficiaries of innovation. This explains the rising gap in wealth between advanced countries and developing countries that import from them.

Chapter 4

Smarter Society

"Changing the world is one, among the many things technology has the power to do"

Modern technology has brought numerous groundbreaking advancements that have revolutionized the way things are done. Big data analysis, fiber optics, artificial intelligence, image recognition, computer softwares, drones and others now have big roles to play in different industrial sectors.

Virtual reality is becoming much more than an entertainment device. Companies now use VR technology in various ways. In the real estate industry for example, some companies have VR solutions that allow potential home buyers walk through every aspect of a home and see every detail of the home right from their living room couch.

Image recognition is currently being used by industries for facial recognition, video analysis, driverless vehicles, augmented reality (AR), surveillance etc.

Drones are now used in modernized hospitals to deliver supplies to various floors. Farmers now use drones to monitor their farms and detect pests, diseased crops, and other important things faster. Drones are being used in the entertainment industry to creatively entertain people and form pyrotechnic displays. Large warehouses are now being monitored by using drones.

Technology has gone beyond the usual manufacturing, aerospace, automotive, electronics, shipbuilding, telecommunication, computer, software industries etc. Technologies that are emerging into prominence will exert considerable impact on the socio-economic domains for decades to come. This prompted Professor Klaus Schwab into introducing the phrase "Fourth Industrial Revolution"

Previously distinct fields are in some ways moving towards stronger interconnection and similar goals. This brings technological convergence to play. Convergence brings previously separate technologies together so they share resources and interact with each other, creating new efficiencies.

Automation, Geo-spatial tech, autonomous vehicles, cloud computing, wireless power, faster and better internet (5G, Li-Fi, broadband inclined fiber, LPN and LORA), new touch interfaces, smart cities, edge/fog computing, advanced materials, new screens, quantum computing, human-computer interaction, health tech, nanotechnology, collaborative tech, voice assistant, proximity tech, clean tech, 3D printing, mobile technology, immersive media (VR/AR/MR/360 degree), energy tech, cyber security inclined adaptive security, artificial intelligence, internet of things (IOT), industrial internet of things (IIOT) etc. will impact society, marketplace and culture.

The most prominent impact of emerging technologies, however, lies in the future so they are still somewhat uncertain and ambiguous. If African countries are embracing technology, they should do it holistically by thinking long-term.

Robotic exoskeletons are already in use by the military to give soldiers extra strength and abilities. They could also help disabled people, especially those who are unable to walk or use their arms get about easily. Prosthetic and robotic limbs are already a reality, and have proven invaluable, but to have a whole robotic body would provide a whole new level of freedom for many around the world.

Chapter 5

Africa's Growing Investment Market

"Africa escaped the global decline in foreign direct investment (FDI) as flows to the continent rose to US$46 billion in 2018, an increase of 11% on the previous year, according to UNCTAD's World Investment Report 2019"

Although Foreign Direct Investment in some large economies on the continent such as Nigeria and Egypt shrank, growth in non-resource-seeking investment as well as growing demand for some commodities and a corresponding rise in their prices underpinned a rise in the continent's FDI. The surge in investment flows to other regions, most significantly South Africa, outweighed the decline in some economies. Africa Continental Free Trade Agreement (AfCFTA) signed on 21st March 2018 in Kigali, Rwanda, will further bolster regional cooperation. This is a good sign that Foreign Direct investment will continue to rise.

As the developed world matures, and becomes increasingly difficult to trade in as opportunities for corporate growth becomes limited, Africa and Asia are emerging as the future of the world's growth. Global brands are now in a race to capture developing -world consumers. Africa has become the newest destination for emerging markets investors. From 2000, according to the World Economic Forum, "half of the world's fastest-growing economies have been in Africa." Ghana and Ethiopia showed real GDP growths of over 8% in 2018. The continent also has the advantage of a large and relatively cheap educated labor force.

In North Africa, according to the United Nations, FDI flows climbed by 7% to $14 billion. Investments in Egypt shrank (down by 8% to $6.8 billion), but the country continued to be the largest FDI recipient in Africa. In Morocco, FDI increased by 36% to $3.6 billion on the back of sizeable investments in finance and the automotive sector.

Foreign Direct Investment to West Africa declined by 15%, to $9.6 billion, largely due to Nigeria where flows plunged by 43% to $2 billion. FDI flows to Ghana also dipped, although by a more moderate 8%, to $3 billion.

FDI was steady at $9 billion in East Africa, the fastest-growing region of the continent. Ethiopia topped the region, even as flows to the country declined by 18%, to $3.3 billion. Flows to Kenya moved up by 27% to $1.6 billion, due to investment in diverse sectors, including oil and gas, manufacturing, chemicals, and hospitality.

While Angola remained negative (-$5.7 billion), largely due to oil and gas firms transferring funds to parent companies through intra-company loans, Southern Africa saw the biggest turnaround, with flows recovering to $4.2 billion after net divestment of $925 million the previous year. Largely attributable to intra-company transfers by established investors, FDI in South Africa more than doubled to $5.3 billion.

FDI flows to Sub-Saharan Africa climbed by 13% to $32 billion. Quite a recovery after successive contractions in the two prior years.

Opportunities are much in Africa. For example, across much of sub-Saharan Africa, there are no roads, airports, rails, ports, power grids and proper IT needed to boost African economies. The growth of imports, exports, and regional business are hindered by this lack of infrastructure. Companies that can connect Africans and markets will prosper. Large investment is leading to major upgrades and expansion at African ports and airports, but much of Africa's growth potential depends on roads, rail and air connections linking different countries within the continent and states within individual countries.

The continent's late arrival to the digital economy

could be seen as an opportunity. Africa's rapidly-expanding population is looking to technology to solve an array of problems, left unsolved by existing local companies. Foreign companies are realizing the huge profit that can come up from the continent's digital transformation, and more corporations are scrambling to be a part of the growth story.

The informal economy represents nearly 72% of Africa's economy, and around 38% of regional GDP - from street vendors to artisans, farmers to taxi drivers. For investors and entrepreneurs in Africa's informal economy, opportunities abound for those capable of uniting fragmented markets and using data to improve productivity. There's likely to be greater engagement and investment in large agent networks to bring goods and services to an underpenetrated informal market as e-commerce in Africa develops. Enhanced rollout of infrastructure also paves the way for startups marketing affordable software-as-a-service (SaaS) platforms that will allow informal merchants to have access to the same services as their structured retail partners: simplified accounting portals, point-of-sale systems, access to credit, and inventory management. Similar SaaS will also benefit farmers. Also, more companies will emerge to provide opportunities to benefit from an under-penetrated informal job market through digital platforms like Lynx or Max which provide access to larger customer bases.

Since Sub-Saharan Africa is plagued by power outages (almost 700 hours a year on average), weakening productivity, adding cost and leaving businesses captive to back-up and alternative power options, companies investing in energy can make a fortune.

Chapter 6

Beyond Existing Government Model

"In my vision, I propose a National Commission for Industries Development (NCID) for African countries, funded by revenues from mining of metals and minerals or as decided by the government. This commission will regulate the establishment of startup industries, assess their performances and provide capital to promising industries whose products appear globally competitive".

Africa cannot rely on Foreign Direct Investment to boost its economy. Understanding this isn't about having a degree in micro-economics or being a math wizard - all you need is to comprehend how economics works. Governments need to create policies that encourage citizens to set up industries; light, heavy and high tech industries. There's a large pool of highly-skilled citizens resident outside the continent (and even within) who will be swift to return to their home countries following moves by the government such as the establishment of a National Commission for Industries Development (NCID). Governments should also establish an Authority for Scientific Research.

The National Commission for Industries Development (NCID), in my vision, will also serve as a unit of governments venturing into partnerships with private industry founders. Industrial/technology entrepreneurs who require financial support to bring their big ideas to life can submit proposals to NCID for review, and successful ones, after following due procedures will be required to issue certificates for shares to NCID. This makes the "National Commission for Industries Development" part owner of the business. If properly managed, this will lead to establishment of industries owned jointly by the government and private sectors. It will drive export and boost value-added component of exported goods. Interest of citizens will move towards setting up industries, and citizens with enough capital will set up industries without intervention from governments. Competition in the continent will rise - which is very healthy to drive economic growth. Unsuccessful businesses will fade out of business, leaving globally competitive ones in the race. Priority will be given to certain industries, particularly to those manufacturing import-substituted goods. African countries will begin to spend less on import, and will generate more revenues from exports. This is one of the ways African countries can build industrial economies and become globally competitive.

The education system has a relevant role here. Africa's education system tends to depend on learning by heart rather than on developing creativity and innovation. A sophisticated or high-tech industrial sector for countries requires highly trained and educated labor force. The spread of education, particularly tertiary institutions focused on technology will produce nationals with required skills.

Industry organization is also important. Let's look at Japan and the United States; two advanced economies. Japan has a vertically integrated and hierarchical industrial structure centered on manufacturing. In the US however, building horizontal industrial economy that includes platforms and ecosystems is paramount. Japan's strength has continued to lie in manufacturing. When it comes to services and soft goods (Softwares, contents), it has either failed to produce competitive companies, or these companies have failed to establish themselves in foreign markets. A growing share of global value chains is now captured by services and soft goods, such as software, while the percentage which accrues to manufacturing is declining. In the past 20 years, many of the companies that have been created or grown rapidly have software and information platform at their cores: Online search, information and ecommerce (Amazon, eBay, Bloomberg, Facebook), PC (Operating systems like Windows), the internet (web browsers such as Internet explorer, Safari, Firefox), Digital Media (Apple's IPod and ITunes combination) etc.

There are, for example, no Japanese global

information services companies comparable to Google, Bloomberg and Thomson Reuters, nor is there any truly global Japanese hotel chains. No Japanese corporations compete internationally with UPS, FedEx and DHL. There are no international Japanese consulting or accounting firms. Japanese companies are also absent from international markets in sectors which are very strong at home; sectors like mobile telecommunications and Anime production. Japanese policymakers are beginning to realize this, and may take swift steps towards addressing it.

Chapter 7

Urbanization Strategy

"Poor urban infrastructure reduces cities' economic prospect and competitiveness"

African political leaders need to intentionally build proper infrastructures like roads, ports, power grids, IT backbone, and create policies for massive investment in real estate as well as tourist attraction projects to boost economy. Advanced economies in Europe, North America and Asia have done that for decades. The result was continuous inflow of immigrants, which of course contributes significantly to economic growth. For citizens, more people will migrate from rural areas in addition to natural urban demographic growth. The National Commission for Industries Development (NCID) as part owner of some industries in the country can generate revenue enough to fund this project. Loans from financial institutions should be avoided at any cost.

Needless to add, Governments should draw lessons from US economic slump where a combination of financial innovations and Federal policy to encourage home ownership allowed borrowers who might otherwise not qualify for a loan, to obtain generous home loans with expectations that interest rates will remain low and housing prices will continue to rise indefinitely. As at the time of the recession in 2001, following the World Trade Centre attack of September

11 2001, the Federal Reserve pushed interest rates to the lowest levels seen up to that time in the post-Bretton Woods era. Their aim was to achieve economic stability. Because US Federal Reserve held low interest rates through 2004, combined with government policy that encourages home ownership, US experienced a steep boom in real estate and financial sector.

From 2004 through 2006, the Federal Reserve then increased interest rates steadily in an attempt to maintain stable inflation rate in the economy. Market interest rates rose in response, and flow of new credit through traditional banking model into real estate moderated. The rates on adjustable mortgages at the time, as well as more exotic loans began to reset at much higher rate than many borrowers expected or were led to expect. This led to the Great Recession. The Great Recession was an economic downturn in the United States from 2007 to 2009 after the bursting of US housing bubble. It was the most severe economic recession in the United States since the Great Depression of the 1930s. The US Bureau of Labor statistics reported the recession to have cost the United States 8.7 million jobs, causing unemployment rate to double. The contagion spread to other economies in the world, notably Europe. It ended in June 2009.

The strategy recommended in this chapter will usher rapid development across Africa. Foreign Direct

Investment (FDI) will maintain a record high, standards of living will improve and the continent will be more connected for trade purposes... These are the hallmark of a proper society. Unplanned and unsustainable patterns of urban development make developing cities focal points for many emerging environment and health hazards.

Chapter 8

The African Union

The European Union (EU), while not without flaws, has served its citizens in their best interest. This is something the African Union has failed to do, because of multiple internal irregularities and corruption issues. Daniel Batidam, the Ghanaian who was elected Chairperson of the AU's Advisory Board on Corruption in 2015, before becoming an ordinary board member two years later, resigned before the end of his mandate in 2019. "Enough is enough", Batidam wrote in his resignation letter dated June 8, 2018. He stated that the organization had "multiple irregularities" and that "issues have come up over and over again" regarding corruption. Abuse of power, lack of transparency and accountability. The African Union quickly accepted his resignation, with Batidam saying that it was a sign that mismanagement towards corruption will "continue with business as usual." Batidam wants African leaders to put pressure on the African Union to reform. In his words "It is my hope that they will call on people in high places at the Commission to take responsibility." If they don't, he urges African citizens to question the need for a continental body such as the African Union and its adjoining structures which are taking millions and millions of dollars to keep running. That money could address poverty on the African continent and yet we are using it to finance corruption.

The AU has a population of over 1 billion citizens and is a continental union made up of 55 member states, with a combined GDP (nominal) of over $2 trillion. Official bodies of the African Union includes; Economic, Social and Cultural Council, Pan-African Parliament (PAP), Executive Council, Assembly of the African Union, African Union Commission, Permanent Representatives' Committee, Court of Justice of the African Union, Peace and Security Council, Specialized Technical Committee. In a summit held in Accra, Ghana on July 2007, the AU considered creating a Union Government which can be regarded as aiming towards a United States of Africa. This project has not been completed or may never be completed due to divisions among African states on the proposal. In an effort to achieve greater continental integration, The 1980 Lagos Plan of Action for the Development of Africa and the 1991 treaty to establish the African Economic Community proposed the creation of Regional Economic Communities (REC), with a timetable for regional integration and then continental integration to follow.

There are currently eight RECs recognized by the AU. Each was established under a separate regional treat; the Common Market for Eastern and Southern Africa

(COMESA), the Economic Community of West African States (ECOWAS), the Arab Maghreb Union (AMU), the Southern Africa Development Community (SADC), the Economic Community of Central African States (ECCAS), the East African Community (EAC), the Community of Sahel-Saharan States (CEN-SAD), the Intergovernmental Authority on Development (IGAD).

The AU has a future goal to create policies like free trade area, a central bank, a single market, a customs union, and a common currency. This they hope will establish economic and monetary union. The current plan is to establish an African Economic Community with a single currency by 2023.

All UN member states based in Africa and on African waters are members of the AU, including the disputed Sahrawi Arab Democratic Republic (SADR), even though Morocco claims sovereignty over SADR. Sudan was suspended on 6th June 2019 by the AU over government's alleged mistreatment of protestors. List of member states below;

Algeria

Angola

Benin

Botswana

Burkina Faso

- Burundi
- Cape Verde
- Cameroon
- Central African Republic
- Chad
- Comoros
- Democratic Republic of the Congo
- Djibouti
- Egypt
- Equatorial Guinea
- Eritrea
- Eswatini
- Ethiopia
- Gabon
- Gambia
- Ghana
- Guinea
- Guinea-Bissau
- Ivory Coast

Kenya

Lesotho

Liberia

Libya

Madagascar

Malawi

Mali

Mauritania

Mauritius

Morocco

Mozambique

Namibia

Niger

Nigeria

Republic of the Congo

Rwanda

Sahrawi Arab Democratic Republic

São Tomé and Príncipe

Senegal

Seychelles

Sierra Leone

Somalia

South Africa

South Sudan

Sudan

Tanzania

Togo

Tunisia

Uganda

Zambia

Zimbabwe

Chapter 9

Agriculture: Pre-requisite for raw materials

Nearly all countries started off poor, and advanced countries today, in those days, successfully shifted wealth from agriculture into manufacturing. They went through structural transformation in their economies - from traditional technology to modern technology and from agriculture to industry and manufacturing. Now they all have high-income service economies. East Asia and the Pacific were among the regions that benefited from the Green Revolution between 1960 and 1990 where cereal yield quadrupled but Africa missed out on this period, and its economic growth has in some ways been held back by continuous lack of progress in agricultural productivity. Africa should work to modernize agriculture. Agricultural modernization prepares conditions for industrialization by increasing agricultural surplus to accumulate capital, increasing foreign exchange via exports, and boosting labor productivity. Modernization also helps achieve humanitarian goals by lowering food prices, raising incomes and productivity of poor farmers, and improving nutrition.

Agriculture supplies raw materials to a variety of

industries apart from food and textile industry, her main customers today. Agro-allied Industries depend on raw materials from agriculture to operate successfully in the production of finished goods. Governments can generate revenue from this sector to accelerate economic growth. The beverage industry depends on raw materials like coffee, cocoa and tea. Soap industry depend on oil seed/oil. Tyre industry depend on rubber latex. Paper industry depend on pulp wood. Starch industry depend on cassava and maize. Breweries depend on cereal. Textile and ginnery depend on cotton. Fruit canning industry depend on fruits. Tobacco industry depend on tobacco leaves. Oil milling industry depend on oil seeds. Sugar industry depend on sugar cane. Rapid agricultural transformation occurs when governments invest in agricultural research and development (R&D), and modern technology is made available. The next move would then be adoption of modern technologies, as farmers may not use these technologies even though they are available.

There is urgent need for governments and policy makers to take a critical look into mining-agriculture relationship. Mining occurs in the same geographic areas as agriculture. Both compete for similar inputs, like land, water and labor. This signals that there is a significant risk that agriculture will be adversely affected by mining. They are both vital to the survival of most African economies. They both contribute to export revenues and employ a large number of people.

Chapter 10

Rivers and Economic Value: The Case of Africa

Governments in Africa should embark on cooperative management of international rivers for economic growth, geological stability, and environmental management. Cooperation in international rivers is fundamentally a political activity. However, African countries will pursue joint action if they realize greater benefit holds through cooperation than through unilateral action. An economic perspective will help clarify this.

Africa is characterized by many great rivers, playing essential economic, social, and environmental roles. The continent's rivers, lakes, and wetlands not only serve extensively as avenues for transport, but also supply water for domestic, agricultural, livestock, and industrial use. More than 60 international rivers traverse Africa, according to The World Bank findings. There are at least 34 rivers shared by two countries. 28 of the international rivers are shared by three or more countries. Ten river basins - Congo, Niger, Volta, Limpopo, Nile, Okavango, Ogooue, Orange, Senegal, and Zambezi are shared by four or more African nations. Proper management and use of these waters can create wealth for Africa. As countries become more connected for trade purposes, a fundamental need arises for governments to explore more avenues for transporting products, and sea transportation has proven especially useful. African countries should pursue economically, socially, and environmentally sound investments in river management infrastructure, both nationally and internationally on shared river systems. Such a diversified portfolio of policies and investments requires a thorough understanding of the economic value of water. Every country in Africa has at least one international river within its territorial borders. 41 nations have two or more, and 15 countries have five or more. Guinea has 14 international rivers, Cote d'Ivoire 9, and Mozambique 9. However, the number of international river basins found in individual country poses a challenge, because if joint management of one river basin is a challenge, joint management of many basins by one country is especially difficult. Extensive international diplomacy and multiple political negotiations will have to come in.

Manufacturing and other industries use water during production processes for either cooling equipment used in creating their products or for creating their products. The United States Geological Survey (USGS) points that industrial water is used for fabricating, processing, washing, diluting, cooling, or transporting a product. Petroleum refineries, smelting facilities, and industries producing chemical products, food, and paper products also use water. Large amounts of water are used mostly to produce food, paper, and chemicals. Manufacturing and service industries often prefer locating in areas with sufficient, reliable water supplies. When there are economic incentives for doing so, they adopt water-saving technologies. Fewer enterprises invest where water supply is unreliable, and those that do will often construct their own water supplies, like private boreholes. These independent water supply arrangements raises the cost of production and affect competitiveness and profitability.

According to the United Nations World Water Development Report, industry accounts for 22% of all global water withdrawals. 59% in high-income countries, and 8% in low-income countries. More water is used for Agriculture which accounts for about 50% of freshwater use. Industry tends to use mainly freshwater; saltwater is unsuitable for most applications as it corrodes the metal parts used in machinery. Industry will probably account for 24% of global freshwater withdrawals by 2025. The electric power production industry accounts for 50% to 70% of industrial water use, comprising hydroelectric, nuclear, and coal and oil-fired power stations. Much of industrial water is available for reuse, but it is usually degraded by the processes it has been involved in, and will require treatment before its return to the water supply system.

Chapter 11

Today's Disruptive Technology

A disruptive technology is any enhanced or completely new technology that replaces an existing technology and shakes up the industry. It can also be seen as a ground-breaking product that creates a completely new industry. This type of technology significantly alters the way businesses or entire industries operates. Harvard Business School professor Clayton M. Christensen, is best known for his theory of disruptive innovation first introduced in his 1997 book "The Innovator's Dilemma". In business theory, a disruptive innovation is an innovation that creates a new market and eventually disrupts an existing market. It creates a value network that disrupts an existing value network.

Some of today's disruptive technologies are;

Artificial Intelligence: Artificial intelligence (AI) as a field of computer science is devoted to creating computer systems that perform tasks much like a human, particularly those involving decision-making and learning. The functions of AI includes, but are however not limited to learning, understanding, reasoning, and interaction. The two very distinct types of AI are; narrow and strong. Narrow AI describes computer systems thoroughly proficient at performing specific tasks, such as Apple's virtual assistant, Siri, which interprets voice commands. Strong AI, a hypothetical type of AI that can meet or exceed human-level intelligence, is also referred to as artificial general intelligence (AGI). This type of AI can apply its problem-solving ability to any kind of issue. The notion that AGI is feasible and imminent has created many fears about AI, including the fear that most jobs will be eliminated. However, at least for the foreseeable future, computer systems that can fully mimic the human brain are only going to be found in Hollywood movie scripts - not in the labs in Silicon Valley.

The Internet of Things: The Internet of Things (IoT) describes the concept that the Internet is now also a platform for devices to communicate electronically with the world around them, and no longer merely a global network wherein people communicate with one another using computers. A combination of technologies, including low-cost sensors, scalable cloud computing, low-power processors, and ubiquitous wireless connectivity has enabled IoT. The result is a world that is alive with information as data can now flow from one device to another and can be shared and reused for a multitude of purposes, including analytics. Companies are just beginning to use these technologies to embed sensing capabilities and intelligence in their machines and products, to allow everyday objects to sense, learn from, and interact with their environment. In industry verticals, this is known as 'smart x' (smart manufacturing, smart transportation, smart agriculture, etc.).

Autonomous Devices: Certain mechanical devices have some ability to interact with their environment and change their physical actions in response. They are called autonomous devices. The most widely known autonomous device is the self-driving vehicle - it has the ability to navigate its surroundings partially or completely without human intervention.

Blockchain: Blockchain is a digital-ledger technology. In blockchain technology, immutable transactions are recorded digitally and made available across a network of computers. It enables decentralized generation, storage, and transfer of information. Blockchain technologies have been used for currency (e.g., Bitcoin); digital identification and certification; shipping and supply chain integration, including smart contracts; public records; and financial services. Blockchain technologies is still in its early stages of development.

New Materials: This refers to innovations in physical materials in their entirety. Breakthroughs in chemistry and improvements in nanotechnology have made it easier for engineers to design and mass produce materials with more innovative properties. For example, graphene is a form of carbon consisting of a single layer of atoms arranged into a hexagonal lattice that is also the strongest material ever tested. According to estimate by European Commission, 70 percent of product innovation in the near future will be based on materials that have new or improved properties, and much of this innovation will have important impacts on productivity; especially by extending the lifetime of products. Such materials could be used to make products last much longer (e.g., roofing materials and paint that last 100 years).

Robotics: The term "Robot" generally refers to physical machines that can be programmed to perform a variety of different tasks, with limited or no input from an operator, and with some level of interaction with its environment. The importance of robotics will continue to grow in both services and goods production, just as the number of different technologies that enable production processes to be automated continues to grow. Overall, robots are getting cheaper, more flexible, and more autonomous, in part by incorporating machine learning systems. A robot may look human, or may not. Whether a robot looks like a human is immaterial to its being a robot.

Convergence: Technologies in previously distinct fields are beginning to move towards closer interconnection. Autonomous devices and robots will increasingly rely on artificial intelligence, for example. Nanotechnology and data analytics are being combined with biological innovations to drive biotechnology advances. Going forward, many industries will need shared technological capabilities, such as AI and data analytics, robotics, autonomy, IoT, and other cyber-physical systems. And more skilled workers will be needed in these technical areas.

Chapter 12

Racism Thrive Because No Black Nation is Successful

"If there was any very successful black nation, the world will agree that the failure of the rest of them is not due to the black race being of inferior people. Blacks' humiliation and helplessness all over the world won't end, until Africa has a first world black nation to lift up its people"

The Arabs colonized, enslaved and enforced their religion on tribes and nations during incursion of foreigners into Africa. Then came the Europeans, who pioneered the idea that Africans were of an inferior race. The Europeans carted off a large population of black people; sometimes almost leaving an entire village empty. Those who remained on the continent were brought under their rule. Since then, no black nation retained its ancestral nationhood, national identity or national language. All of Africa's colonial masters left behind a way of life completely decimated, a people traumatized and taught in colonial schools to detest everything about themselves: their skin, their dress, their languages, their customs. Even their gods were replaced. It was a complete transformation, so unforgiving for history.

And today we often hear of how countries like China and India (including many others) are 'taking over' Africa economically. Many nations of a different race have spat on the face of the black person, at one time or the other.

Early African-Americans like Malcolm X, Marcus Garvey and W.E.B Du Bois saw that the future of their race could not be made better by endless protests or marches demanding equality or justice. It is the restoration of the crushed dignity of the black man that can. Great men of those era knew that a people is only respected when it has a nation worthy of respect. They understood that for blacks to reclaim power they must first reclaim dignity. That dignity can only come through the construction of a solid black state with admirable level of development and prosperity, and that can stand as a powerful advocate for the global black. No such state exists today.

Nigeria, the most populous black nation on Earth, has failed to stand up to its responsibility. It is at the verge of collapse, as the machineries that makes a nation exists - let alone succeed, have all been eroded. A long-standing culture of incompetence, endemic corruption, selfishness and greed on the side of its leaders has kept the country on backward trend. Many other African countries are no different. Because there are no healthy black nations, and African and Caribbean countries lie in the midst of chaos, corrupted religiosity, violence, senseless wars, and economic collapse, African and Caribbean people leave home en masse. They prostitute in the red-light zones of the Netherlands, beg on the streets of Greece, and make up 40 percent of the migrants flocking to Europe. As they make their way to these countries; unwanted, helpless, starved, or maimed, they are treated like dogs.

At 16, I disliked the reality that I was African. I became eager to travel to the United States, giving up my Nigerian nationality to take up an American since nothing works as it should in Nigeria. It was until I was 21 that I realized I needed to stay to build Nigeria, working with fellow Nigerians. At the time I rounded up secondary education, I never applied to take up tertiary education in Nigeria or other African countries. I turned in my application to Michigan State University in the United States for 3 consecutive years as it was my most preferred institution globally, yet things never worked out. Next, I applied to University of Toronto in Canada, University of Edinburgh in UK, University of Tokyo in Japan and some others. The effort yielded no result. All these was entirely an attempt to leave Africa and take up foreign citizenship elsewhere. However, that would have been a terrible mistake for me if I had successfully pulled through my plans to leave Nigeria. At 21, I began to see the need to work with other Africans to build up Africa. Europeans built up Europe. Americans built up North America. Now it's time that we build up Africa. Individual effort counts; to this end, I became determined to contribute my quota.

Early in 2018, I watched Prof Kingsley Moghalu declare to run for the presidency of Nigeria. I admired his boldness and demonstrable level of competence, so I signed up. I was one of those who worked very closely with him during his presidential campaign in Nigeria's 2019 election. The election was lost to President Mohammadu Buhari. Time passed quickly, and I approached Prof Kingsley Moghalu with an idea after the election; he shared in the idea and agreed to work with me. Engr. Dr. Donald Igwegbu who was a presidential aspirant signed up as well. We registered SperaDeal Global Nigeria Limited in Abuja - Nigeria's capital city. We were inspired to meet Africa's technology demand by setting up industries; manufacturing tech products and providing services that solves problems. Much has been done so far, but we are constantly open to absorbing young, innovative and technology-minded Africans. We hope to work with them to build the largest technology company in Africa. Prof Akii Ibhadode, the Vice Chancellor of Federal University of Petroleum Resources Effurun joined our team months later, while Prof Kingsley Moghalu withdrew.

In my opinion, Africa will experience rapid technological and economic transformation if young and competent citizens occupy policymaking arms of government across the continent. It has been my dream to see this happen, and it will happen. We must push for policies that can transform the continent. Young Nigerians will offer less corrupt political leadership than our current political establishment who care only about themselves. This is why I've always encouraged young, well-meaning Nigerians to aspire for offices in Nigeria's National Assembly.

Chapter 13

Global Economy Puzzle and Africa

The world's rich countries continued to grow faster than poorer countries for over 200 years. In 1776 when Adam Smith wrote the Wealth of Nations, per capita income in the world's richest country - probably the Netherlands, was about 4 times that of the poorest countries. Two centuries later, the Netherlands was about 40 times richer than China, and 10 times richer than Thailand. But, over the past three decades, the trend reversed. The Netherlands is now only about 5 times richer than China and 7 times richer than Thailand.

For African countries, while the Netherlands was 7.7 times richer than Côte D' ivoire and 15 times richer than Kenya in 1980, today, it is 30.87 times and 30.96 times richer respectively.

The analysis above presents a clear view that Asian countries are developing at competitive paces in relation to the Western world in recent times. Why can't African countries? After all, shouldn't laggards grow faster than leaders if all they have to do is imitate others? Even leapfrogging technologies that are now obsolete? Ricardo Haussmann queried. In the case of Asian countries, why didn't they grow faster for so long? And why are they doing so now? He added. Obviously, the Asians have learnt from the Western world.

The century is for Asia, but Africa can follow behind closely. Asian economic success is more easily replicable for African countries than that of the West. Many of Africa's policymakers have watched Asian countries rise to economic boom in their lifetime and can move their countries to prosperity through lessons learned from the Asians. Singapore, Hong Kong, Taiwan, and South Korea - the four Asian Tigers, have not always been successful. They rose to prominence in the boom years starting from the 1960s (mid 1950s for Hong Kong) by taking advantage of emerging technology and globalization. The global economy was just starting to recover after the Second World War and the Korean War of 1950 - 1953. Peace as at the time combined with significant advances in air travel and telecommunication signaled that borders were beginning to open. Singapore, South Korea, Hong Kong and Taiwan were perfectly positioned to benefit. These countries have long-established ports and developed trade economies, highly educated population, and a robust post-colonial infrastructure. The governments of the four Asian Tigers took this opportunity, heavily invested in industrialization, built industrial estates, offered tax incentives to foreign investors, and implemented compulsory education for its young population in order to secure the future of the workforce. Today, Hong Kong and Singapore are widely regarded as two of the world's most influential financial hubs (they diversified away from the export market into financial services), while Taiwan and South Korea are home to some of the biggest names in cutting-edge technologies and electronics.

Chapter 14

A note to Africa's aspiring entrepreneurs

Entrepreneurs in Africa are surrounded by more opportunities than they often realize. Much of Africa remains undeveloped, leaving the continent with more problems yet unsolved than (arguably) any other continent in the world. If that is true, entrepreneurs in Africa can grow businesses and create wealth for themselves and the continent by applying creative methods and innovations to solve perceived problems. You'll find that challenges abound especially for technology entrepreneurs due to few available local capabilities relating to cutting-edge technologies, but global production chain has evolved over the years allowing governments and companies to have components of their products manufactured in countries with required expertise, or have their products assembled in a different country, then have the final product sent back. A good illustration of that is Foxconn, a Taiwanese company that manufactures electronic products for major American, Canadian, Finnish, Chinese and Japanese companies. Notable products manufactured by Foxconn include the iPhone, iPad, BlackBerry, iPod, Kindle, Nokia devices, Nintendo 3DS, Xiaomi devices, PlayStation 3, PlayStation 4, Wii U, Xbox 360, Xbox One, and the TR4 CPU socket on some motherboards.

Often, when an average African hears of entrepreneurship, what comes to mind is merely buying and selling, or provision of services using already established system. Entrepreneurship in the real sense goes beyond that into problem-solving. The items we trade with today, and the services and soft goods we enjoy are available because someone envisaged a need to create them. Creating new products to solve problems not only generate wealth for those who brought about them, but also provide job for millions who serve as middle-men and retailers in the distribution chain, and because the highest employer of labor in any country is the private sector, unemployment will drop. The more successful African citizens become, the wealthier the continent becomes overall, as governments boost revenue through taxes.

I had a goal when I enrolled to study Chemical Engineering at the Federal University of Petroleum Resources, Effurun. I was desirous to solve the problem of poor electricity supply in Nigeria by investing heavily in geothermal electricity generation. Geothermal power is generated by geothermal energy. It uses technologies like dry steam power stations, flash steam power stations and binary cycle power stations and is considered to be a sustainable, renewable source of energy because the heat extraction is small compared with the Earth's heat content. Its source is the almost unlimited amount of heat generated by the Earth's core, and it is clean; energy can be extracted without burning a fossil fuel such as coal, gas, or oil. This type of energy is available 24 hours a day, 365 days a year. I understood that to actualize this goal, I'll have to work with foreign companies since there are very few locally available capabilities. Geothermal electricity generation has continued to be one core area of interest for me when it comes to investment, and SperaDeal Global Nigeria Limited (a company where I am the CEO) will work to execute my plans.

To those passionate about entrepreneurship; find out where the problem spots are; single out one (or some) of them; then prepare a business philosophy that solves that problem. If that has been done, CONGRATULATIONS!!! Take any opportunity to network and learn from more experienced executives. Get mentored and coached by them. Expose yourself to specific meetings and boardroom discussions. Learn with a team.

www.ingramcontent.com/pod-product-compliance
Lightning Source LLC
Chambersburg PA
CBHW020615220526
45463CB00006B/2592